GW01396061

CATS REACT

to DINOSAUR FACTS

By Izzi Howell

WAYLAND

First published in Great Britain in 2023 by Wayland
Copyright © Hodder and Stoughton Limited, 2023

ISBN: 978 1 5263 2226 5 (HB)
       978 1 5263 2244 9 (PB)

Produced for Wayland by
White-Thomson Publishing Ltd
www.wtpub.co.uk

Editor: Izzi Howell and Paul Rockett
Designer: Clare Nicholas

Printed in Dubai

Wayland
An imprint of
Hachette Children's Group
Part of Hodder & Stoughton
Carmelite House
50 Victoria Embankment
London EC4Y 0DZ

An Hachette UK Company
www.hachette.co.uk
www.hachettechildrens.co.uk

MIX
Paper from
responsible sources
FSC® C104740
www.fsc.org

The publisher would like to thank the following for permission to reproduce their pictures:

Alamy: Stocktrek Images, Inc. 20b, The Natural History Museum 40r, Stocktrek Images, Inc. 46r and 97t, Mohamad Haghani 92b; Getty: ilterriorm 88l; iStock: sdominick 31l, leonello 38–39c, ilbusca 41b, MR1805 60, milehightraveler 101l; Martin Bustamente 36t, 44, 98–99; NASA/JPL 73bl; Science Photo Library: JAIME CHIRINOS 93l; Shutterstock: Eric Isselee cover, OlgaBartashevich, Artem Furman, Seregraff, Sonsedska Yuliia and Jagodka back cover, Elenarts and Anton27 2t and 81c, Kuttelvaserova Stuchelova 2b, Svyatoslav Balan 3t and 52b, Susan Schmitz 3b and 6t, vvvita 4t and 112, Warpaint and Nynke van Holten 4b, Herschel Hoffmeyer 5tl, 6–7c, 8–9c, 9b, 35t, 58c and 75, Warpaint 5tr, 16l, 25b, 49c, 59, 71t, 76, 87t and 90t, RamonaS 5b, Elenarts 6b, photomaster 7t, Ukki Studio 7b, Tony Campbell 8t, nattanan726 8b, art nick 9t, fufu10 9c, Krunja 9b, Captainz, Iryna Kuznetsova and Bodor Tivadar 10, Ermolaev Alexander, keeella, Warpaint and PixelSquid3d 11, Dina Photo Stories 12l, Dotted Yeti 13, 26, 67r, 84t and 88r,

Marko Aliaksandr 14t, Billion Photos 14b, Sonsedska Yuliia 15l, sruilk 15r, DenisNata 16r, Iryna Kuznetsova, Daniel Eskridge and Atmosphere1 17t, Bachkova Natalia 17b, Catmando and Ermolaev Alexander 18t, Daniel Eskridge 18b, 28t, 32–33c, 34t, 51, 52t and 56–57c, Valentyna Chukhlyebova 19tl, 21t, 95r, 104tl, 104bl and 105tl, cynoclub 19tr and 21b, Natasha Zakharova 19b, Lena Miava 20t, Iryna Kuznetsova 22t, 48l, 74, 77l, 89tl, 93r and 98b, Catmando 22–23c, 31r, 42t and 54, Tuzemka 23r, rodos studio FERHAT CINAR 24l, Eric Isselee 24r, 28b, 29t, 30b, 37b, 46l, 65t, 80b, 97b, 101r, 103, 105tr and 109, Kruglov_Orda 25t, AKKHARAT JARUSILAWONG, Eric Isselee, Cre8tive Images and Ermolaev Alexander 27, Linn Currie 29b, Oksana Kuzmina and Susan Schmitz 29t, Wlad74 30t, Nils Jacobi 33, Viorel Sima 34b, Andrey_Kuzmin 35b, NYU Studio 36b, AKKHARAT JARUSILAWONG 37t, Ermolaev Alexander 39b, 99t, 105bl and 106r, Martina Osmy 40l, Jiri Hera and Marina Swarre 41t, Sonsedska Yuliia and HomeArt 42b, eAlisa 43r, BBA Photography 44–45, MirasWonderland 45t, Richard Peterson 45b, Joshua Haviv 46–47, Nynke van Holten 47t, 70t and 106l, paula French 47b, Ralf Juergen Kraft 48r and 50t, patpitchaya 49t, Matis75 49b, yevgeniy11 50b, Dzha33 53t, Theera Disayarat and milatiger 53b, Stephanie Zieber 55t and 108, oksana2010 55bl and 110t, gritsalak karalak and New Africa 55br, Olgysha 57t, topdigipro and fotogiunta 57c, Popel Arseniy 58r, Rasulov 58b, Volodymyr Krasyuk 61t, Africa Studio 61b, DM7 62t and 68c, Dioniya 62b, Orla 64–65c, Irina Kononova 66l, dimair 66r, Anton27 67t, LilKar and Happy monkey 67l, Potapov Alexander 68t, artemisphoto 68b, David Herraez Calzada and Sarawut Aiemsinsuk 69, rodos studio FERHAT CINAR 70b, Kestutis Jonaitis 71bl, Zaretska Olga 71br, andrea crisante 72t, Oliver Denker 72b, Suzanne Tucker 73tl and 111, Vivienstock 73r, YuRi Photolife 77r, Michael Rosskothen 78l, 80t and 89tr, LifetimeStock 78r, 5 second Studio 79t, Happy monkey 79b, Gelpi 81t, Ndanko 81b and 110b, Konstantin G 82t, BLACKDAY 82b, Esteban De Armas 83t, FotoYakov 83b, Katrina Brown 84b, Morphart Creation 85t, Ales Munt 85b, Seregraff and Serge Pyun 86t, Lefteris Papaulakis 86b, nevodka 87b, Susan Schmitz 89b, Kurit afshen and Linn Currie 90b, Eric Isselee, Ermolaev Alexander, David Carillet and FotoYakov 91, Utekhina Anna 92t, ryazanovm 94l, Nicolas Primola 94r, Utekhina Anna 95l, Natalia van D 96r, chrisbrignell 96b, Oksana Kuzmina 99b, Sharomka 100t, Martina Osmy, Alex Coan and DM7 100b, Sonsedska Yuliia, Bjoern Wylezich and ntv 102, Ansis Klucis 103c, kurhan 103b, Pavel Hlystov 104tr, Dzha33 104br, freestyle images 105br; Wikimedia: Falconaumanni 12r, Didier Descouens 43l.

Cats React cats from Shutterstock: Lubava, Seregraff, Jagodka and Getty: GlobalP, Arseniy45.

All design elements from Shutterstock.

Every attempt has been made to clear copyright. Should there be any inadvertent omission please apply to the publisher for rectification.

CONTENTS

DINOSAURS ARE AMAZING!

The word **DINOSAUR** means **FEARFULLY GREAT LIZARD**! It was **FIRST USED** in 1842.

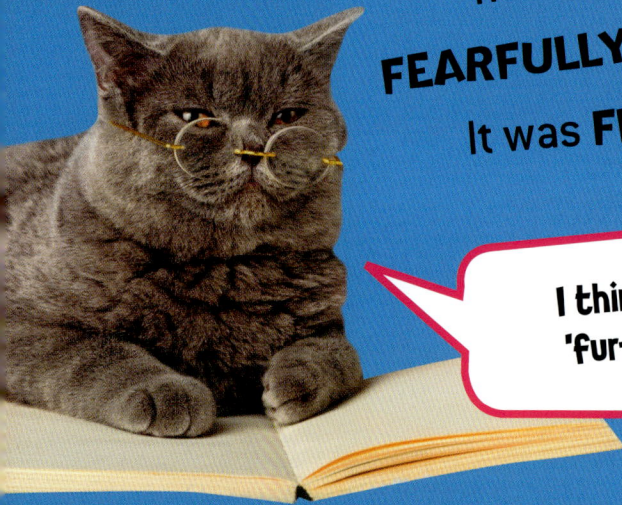

I think you mean 'fur-fully great'!

The **ANCESTORS** of some **DINOSAURS** are **STILL ALIVE TODAY**! **BIRDS EVOLVED** from **SMALL MEAT-EATING DINOSAURS** called **THEROPODS**.

Many dinosaurs had feathers. The feathered dinosaur *Microraptor* may have been able to fly!

Discover **ROAR-SOME DINOSAUR FACTS** and **LAUGH** along with these **CRAZY CAT REACTIONS!** Do you **AGREE** with the **REACT-O-METER?**

If the **HISTORY OF EARTH** was **SHRUNK DOWN** into just **ONE DAY**, the **DINOSAURS** would **ARRIVE AT 10:40PM** and would **LEAVE AT 11:40PM**. The **FIRST HUMAN ANCESTORS** wouldn't appear until **11:58PM!**

It was just an hour, but we made it count!

Prehistoric party time!

← Tyrannosaurus

Diplodocus ↗

Call this a party?

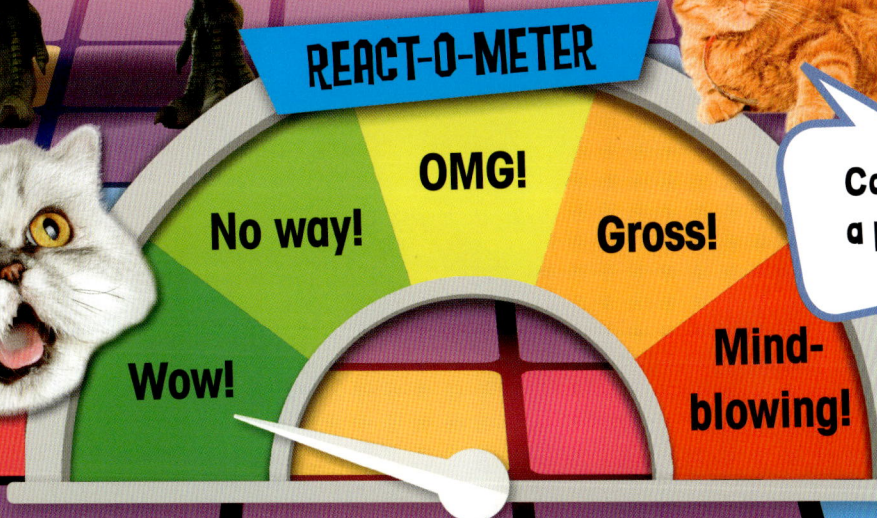

REACT-O-METER

No way!

OMG!

Gross!

Wow!

Mind-blowing!

S

WHAT IS A DINOSAUR?

DINOSAURS are **PREHISTORIC CREATURES** that lived **MILLIONS OF YEARS AGO**.

Prehistoric power!

Dinosaurs ruled the **EARTH** for more than **140 MILLION YEARS**. They were a type of **REPTILE**, like **SNAKES** and **LIZARDS** today.

Compsognathus was only about as large as a chicken, but it was still a fierce predator.

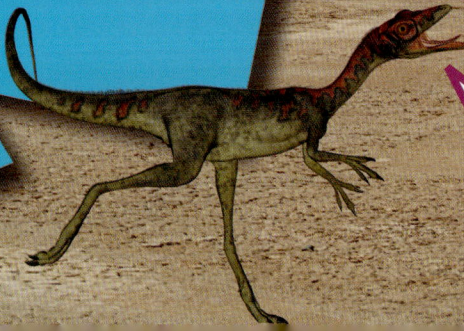

Who says chickens can't be fur-ocious?

Dinosaurs came in many **DIFFERENT SHAPES** and **SIZES**.

Some had **BODIES** as **LARGE** as **BUSES**, while others were as **SMALL** as **PIGEONS**.

You're pretty small for a dino.

Argentinosaurus is thought to have measured 30 m long, which is as long as a blue whale!

Meowza! That's a big one!

Most **MEAT-EATING (CARNIVOROUS)** dinosaurs walked on **TWO LEGS.** Large **PLANT-EATING (HERBIVOROUS)** dinosaurs walked on **ALL FOURS.**

Who are you calling a plant eater?!

Tyrannosaurus

A dinosaur's **LEGS** were positioned **DIRECTLY UNDERNEATH** its body. This is **DIFFERENT** to **MODERN REPTILES,** such as **CROCODILES.** The legs of modern reptiles **STICK OUT TO THE SIDES.**

Stick out? Excuse me! I look fabulous!

Dinosaurs were covered in **SCALES**. Some dinosaurs had **FEATHERS**.

Feathers, just like moi!

CARNIVOROUS dinosaurs had **SHARP, POINTED TEETH** for **SLICING** and **TEARING** through **MEAT**.

We're tooth twins!

Alamosaurus

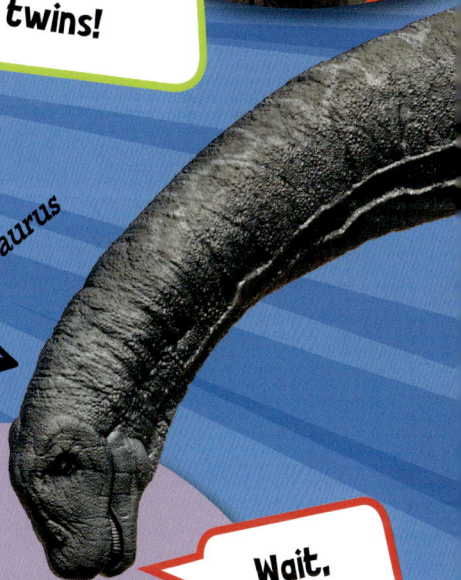

BABY DINOSAURS hatched from **EGGS**.

Wait, what?!

THE AGE OF THE DINOSAURS

LIFE ON EARTH was very DIFFERENT when the DINOSAURS were ALIVE!

The **DINOSAURS** lived during a **TIME** called the **MESOZOIC ERA**. Scientists divide the **MESOZOIC ERA** into **THREE PARTS**: the **TRIASSIC PERIOD** (252 to 201 million years ago), the **JURASSIC PERIOD** (201 to 145 million years ago) and the **CRETACEOUS PERIOD** (145 to 66 million years ago).

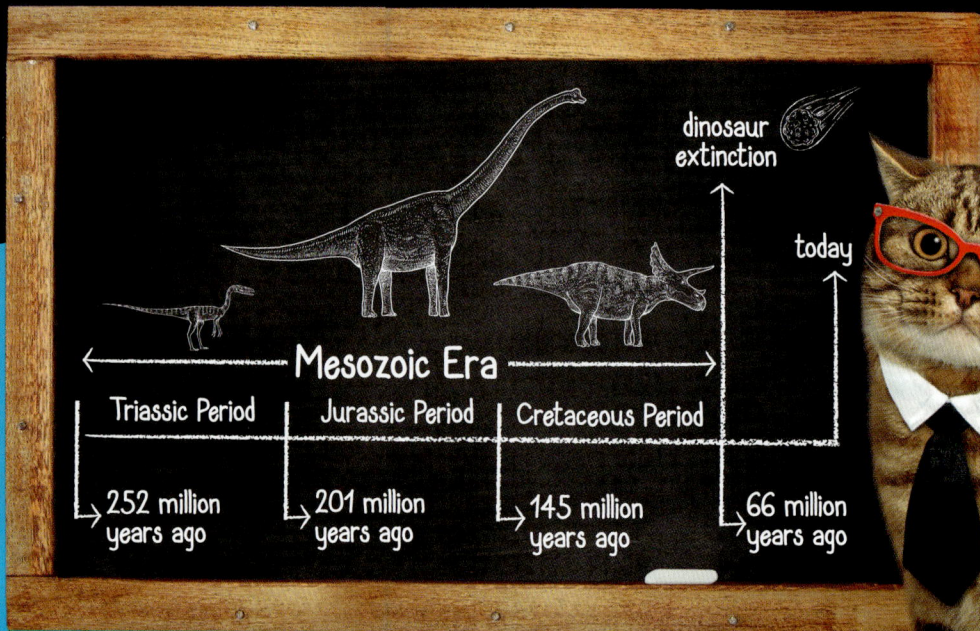

dinosaur extinction

today

Mesozoic Era

| Triassic Period | Jurassic Period | Cretaceous Period |

252 million years ago

201 million years ago

145 million years ago

66 million years ago

People often think that **ALL THE DINOSAURS** lived together at the **SAME TIME,** but this **WASN'T THE CASE.** **DIFFERENT** species of **DINOSAUR** lived in each **PERIOD.** Many species lived **MILLIONS OF YEARS APART.**

Stegosaurus lived in the Late Jurassic Period, around 80 million years before *Ankylosaurus*, which lived in the Late Cretaceous Period!

Ankylosaurus

Stegosaurus

Is this my close-up?

Cat — I mean cut! This is all wrong for Purr-rassic Park!

The LAND, WEATHER and LIFE on EARTH changed a lot during the MESOZOIC ERA.

At the beginning of the TRIASSIC PERIOD, all of the LAND was JOINED TOGETHER, making ONE HUGE CONTINENT called PANGAEA. The FIRST DINOSAURS EVOLVED during this period.

My house is where?

During the **JURASSIC PERIOD, PANGAEA SPLIT APART** into **TWO MAIN CONTINENTS.** The **WEATHER** got **WARMER. DINOSAURS** became the **MOST IMPORTANT LAND ANIMALS.**

WE'RE NUMBER ONE!

Dilophosaurus

In the **CRETACEOUS PERIOD**, the **CONTINENTS** continued to **SPLIT APART** and moved **CLOSER** to their **CURRENT LOCATIONS**.

This **TIME PERIOD** ended with a **CATASTROPHIC EVENT** that **KILLED NEARLY ALL THE DINOSAURS** (see pages 70–75).

Time's up guys!

What is this newfangled red thing?

FLOWERS DIDN'T EXIST ON EARTH UNTIL THE CRETACEOUS PERIOD! BEFORE FLOWERS APPEARED, PLANTS REPRODUCED WITH SPORES OR CONES THAT CONTAINED SEEDS.

Ferns are one of the few modern plants that still reproduce with spores.

No way!

OMG!

Gross!

Wow!

Mind-blowing!

TYPES OF DINOSAUR

We can **SORT DINOSAURS** with **SIMILAR CHARACTERISTICS** into **SEVERAL DIFFERENT GROUPS**.

Allosaurus

usually carnivores

sharp teeth

Many **THEROPODS** were **FIERCE PREDATORS**. This group includes *Tyrannosaurus, Spinosaurus, Allosaurus* and *Velociraptor*.

large claws

walked on two legs

Eeek!

Brachiosaurus

long neck

herbivore

long tail

walked on four legs

SAUROPODS, such as *Diplodocus*, *Apatosaurus* and *Brachiosaurus*, were **GENTLE GIANTS**.

I swear I just saw a giant horse!

17

ORNITHOPODS include *Iguanodon*, *Hadrosaurus* and *Parasaurolophus*.

Get your own dinner!

beak

Parasaurolophus

teeth for grinding plants

walked on two legs but sometimes stood on four legs to eat

Pachycephalosaurus and other members of the **PACHYCEPHALOSAUR** group are well known for their **DISTINCTIVE BIG HEADS!** Some species only ate **PLANTS**, while others were probably **OMNIVORES** (ate PLANTS and MEAT).

Pachycephalosaurus

herbivore or omnivore

thick skull

bony dome

walked on two legs

Nice hat!

ARMOURED DINOSAURS had different types of PROTECTION against PREDATORS, including BONY PLATES and SPIKES. Some were COVERED in plates, while others only had plates along their BACK and TAIL.

Kentrosaurus

herbivore

bony plates

Backing ... ... away ... very ... slowly ...

walked on four legs

You're my fur-shion inspiration!

19

The most famous **CERATOPSIAN** is *Triceratops*. Other **MEMBERS** of this group include *Styracosaurus* and *Albertaceratops*.

I don't know, it looks much better on you!

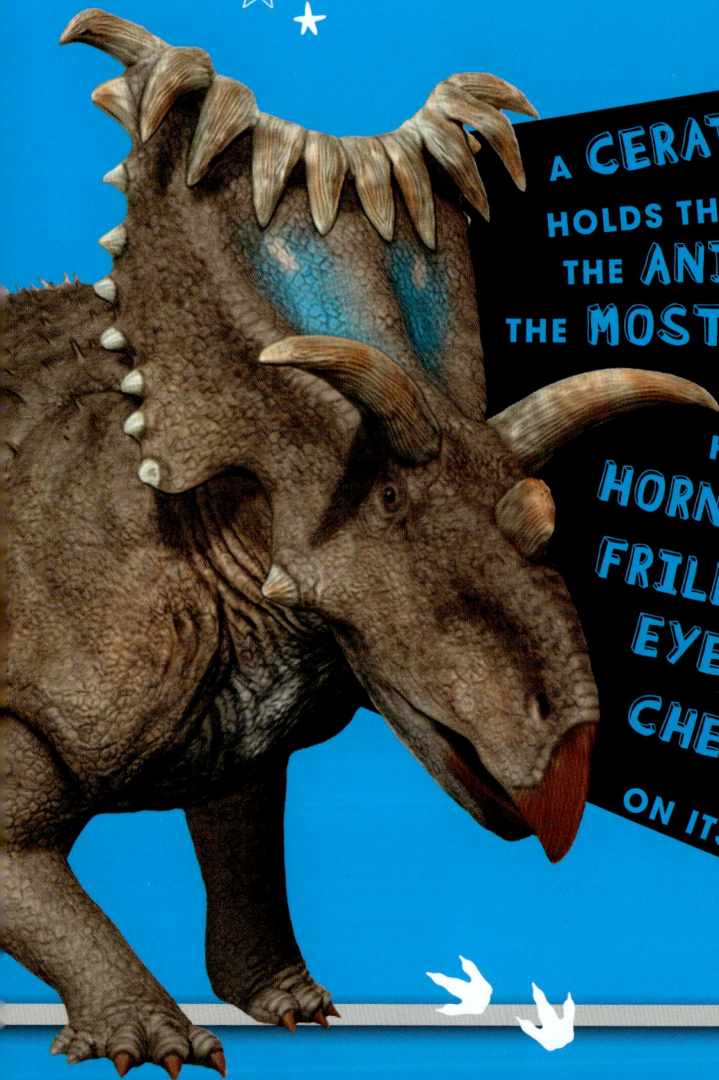

A CERATOPSIAN HOLDS THE RECORD FOR THE ANIMAL WITH THE MOST HORNS EVER! KOSMOCERATOPS HAD FIFTEEN HORNS - TEN ON ITS FRILL, ONE ABOVE EACH EYE, ONE ON EACH CHEEK AND ONE ON ITS NOSE!

Albertaceratops

often had horns

herbivore

big bony neck frill

beak

walked on four legs

Stop it, you look fabulous!

Where are the other fourteen going to fit?

Wow!

No way!

OMG!

Gross!

Mind-blowing!

COELOPHYSIS

Ready to spot some miow-vellous dinos?

COELOPHYSIS was a **SMALL** but **SPEEDY** dinosaur!

Coelophysis was an **EARLY THEROPOD**. Its **SMALL SIZE** meant that it was much **LOWER** down the **FOOD CHAIN** than **LATER, LARGER THEROPODS**. But it was still a fierce **PREDATOR** of **SMALL REPTILES** and **EARLY MAMMALS**.

84, 85, 86 ... SO many teeth!

Coelophysis's **SPEED** and **AGILITY** helped it to catch its prey. It had a **FLEXIBLE NECK** that could **REACH INSIDE BURROWS** and **TWIST** to **SNAP UP ITS PREY** as it was **ESCAPING**. Its **LONG JAWS** were filled with **HUNDREDS OF SHARP TEETH**.

Many **FOSSILISED COELOPHYSIS** have been found together in the **SAME PLACE**. Some **PALAEONTOLOGISTS** believe that this is because *Coelophysis* **LIVED IN GROUPS** and **HUNTED AS A PACK** to **KILL LARGER PREY**.

You go for the tail, I'll take the ears!

HISSSSSS!

However, some **EXPERTS** believe that these **FOSSILS AREN'T ENOUGH EVIDENCE** that *Coelophysis* **LIVED TOGETHER**. They could have **GATHERED TOGETHER** for other reasons, such as **DRINKING** from a **WATER HOLE**, and then been **SUDDENLY KILLED** by a **FLASH FLOOD**.

Order, order!

EXPERTS ONCE BELIEVED THAT COELOPHYSIS WAS A CANNIBAL! THEY FOUND WHAT THEY BELIEVED TO BE A SMALL COELOPHYSIS BONE INSIDE THE STOMACH OF ANOTHER COELOPHYSIS. BUT IT TURNED OUT TO BE THE BONE OF AN EARLY TYPE OF CROCODILE!

I'm innocent, promise!

Wow!

No way!

OMG!

Gross!

Mind-blowing!

ARCHAEOPTERYX

ARCHAEOPTERYX was one of the **FIRST DINOSAURS** with **BIRD-LIKE FEATURES.**

This **MAGPIE-SIZED DINOSAUR** had **WINGS** and **FEATHERS,** just like a **MODERN BIRD.** However, it also had **FEATURES** of a **DINOSAUR,** including **TEETH,** a **LONG BONY TAIL** and **CLAWS** on its **WINGS. MODERN BIRDS** don't have any of these **THINGS.**

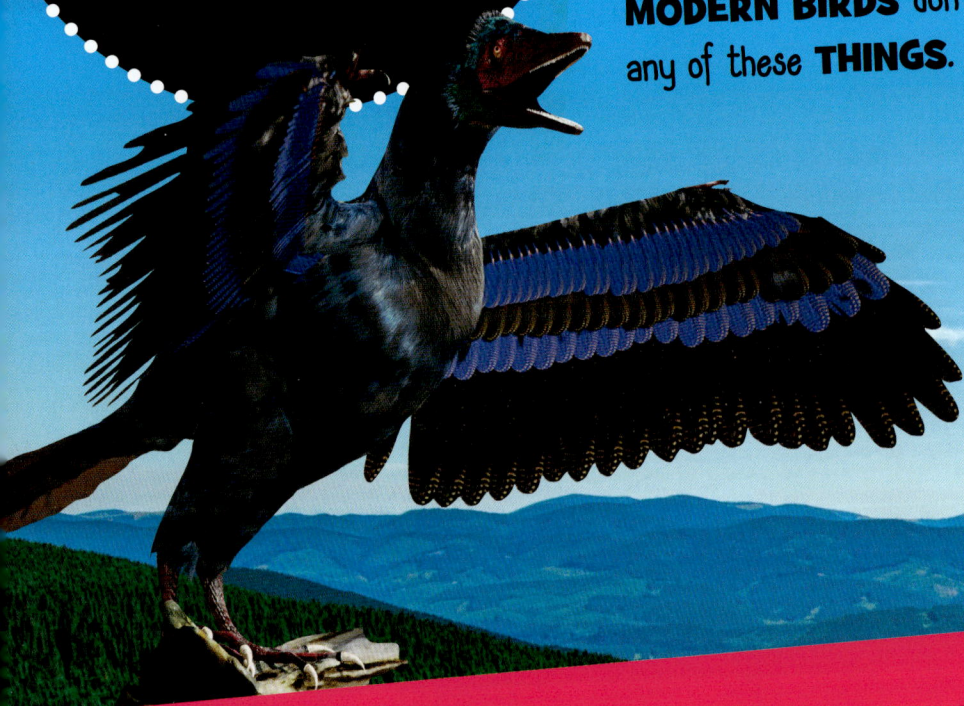

ARCHAEOPTERYX didn't have the **RIGHT SKELETON STRUCTURE** to **FLAP ITS WINGS** and **FLY** long distances, but it could probably **FLY IN SHORT BURSTS** while **HUNTING.**

FACT FILE

LIVED: Late Triassic Period
LENGTH: 0.5 m
WEIGHT: 27 kg

WHEN THE FIRST ARCHAEOPTERYX FOSSILS WERE FOUND IN 1861, SCIENTISTS WERE VERY SURPRISED. THEY HAD NEVER SEEN A DINOSAUR WITH FEATHERS BEFORE. SOME PEOPLE THOUGHT IT MIGHT BE A FOSSILISED ANGEL!

Paw-sitively angelic!

No way!

OMG!

Gross!

Wow!

Mind-blowing!

27

DIPLODOCUS

DIPLODOCUS had such a **LONG NECK** and **TAIL** that it was **LONGER** than a **TENNIS COURT!**

Diplodocus had **15 BONES** in its **LONG NECK**. Some of its **NECK BONES** measured over **1 M!**

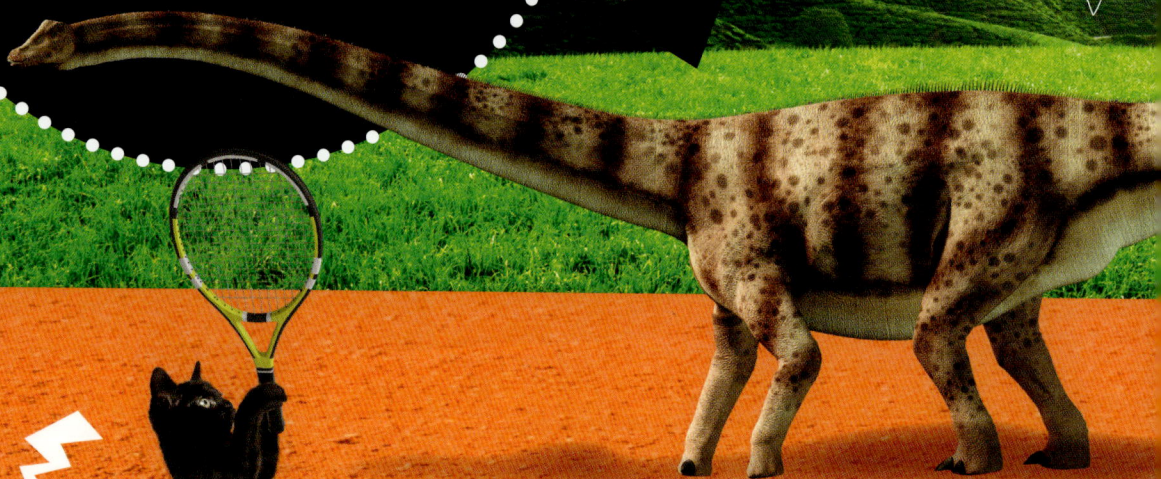

Diplodocus's **GIANT NECK** allowed it to **REACH HIGH LEAVES**. It could also **DROP ITS NECK DOWN** to the ground to **DRINK WATER**.

Diplodocus **HELD UP** its **LONG TAIL** to **BALANCE THE WEIGHT** of its neck. Its tail was **VERY FLEXIBLE.**

Can we play?

Some palaeontologists believe that *Diplodocus* could **CRACK ITS TAIL** like **A WHIP** to **SCARE** or even **ATTACK PREDATORS.**

Hey, we're tail twins!

DIPLODOCUS, like all other **SAUROPODS,** was a **HERBIVORE.** It **HAD SPECIALISED FRONT TEETH** that worked like a **COMB** to separate **LEAVES** from **BRANCHES. EATING** and **GATHERING PLANTS** quickly **WORE DOWN** *Diplodocus's* teeth and so they **FELL OUT** and were **REPLACED** roughly every **35 DAYS!**

Eat up dino, you're nothing but bones!

Amateur!

DIPLODOCUS'S NECK WAS THREE TIMES LONGER THAN THAT OF A GIRAFFE!

Some dinosaurs had EVEN LONGER NECKS than DIPLODOCUS! MAMENCHISAURUS'S NECK made up nearly HALF THE LENGTH of its BODY!

Wow!

No way!

OMG!

Gross!

Mind-blowing!

STEGOSAURUS

STEGOSAURUS was a SLOW, GENTLE HERBIVORE with a SPIKY SECRET WEAPON!

Stegosaurus is WELL KNOWN for the DIAMOND-SHAPED PLATES that ran along its BACK and TAIL. Although they were MADE OF BONE, STEGOSAURUS'S PLATES were SET INTO ITS SKIN, rather than connected to its SKELETON.

Experts AREN'T SURE why *Stegosaurus* had PLATES. They may have made it LOOK SCARY TO PREDATORS or HELPED TO CONTROL ITS BODY TEMPERATURE. The skin that covered *Stegosaurus*'s plates may have been able to CHANGE COLOUR to ATTRACT A MATE.

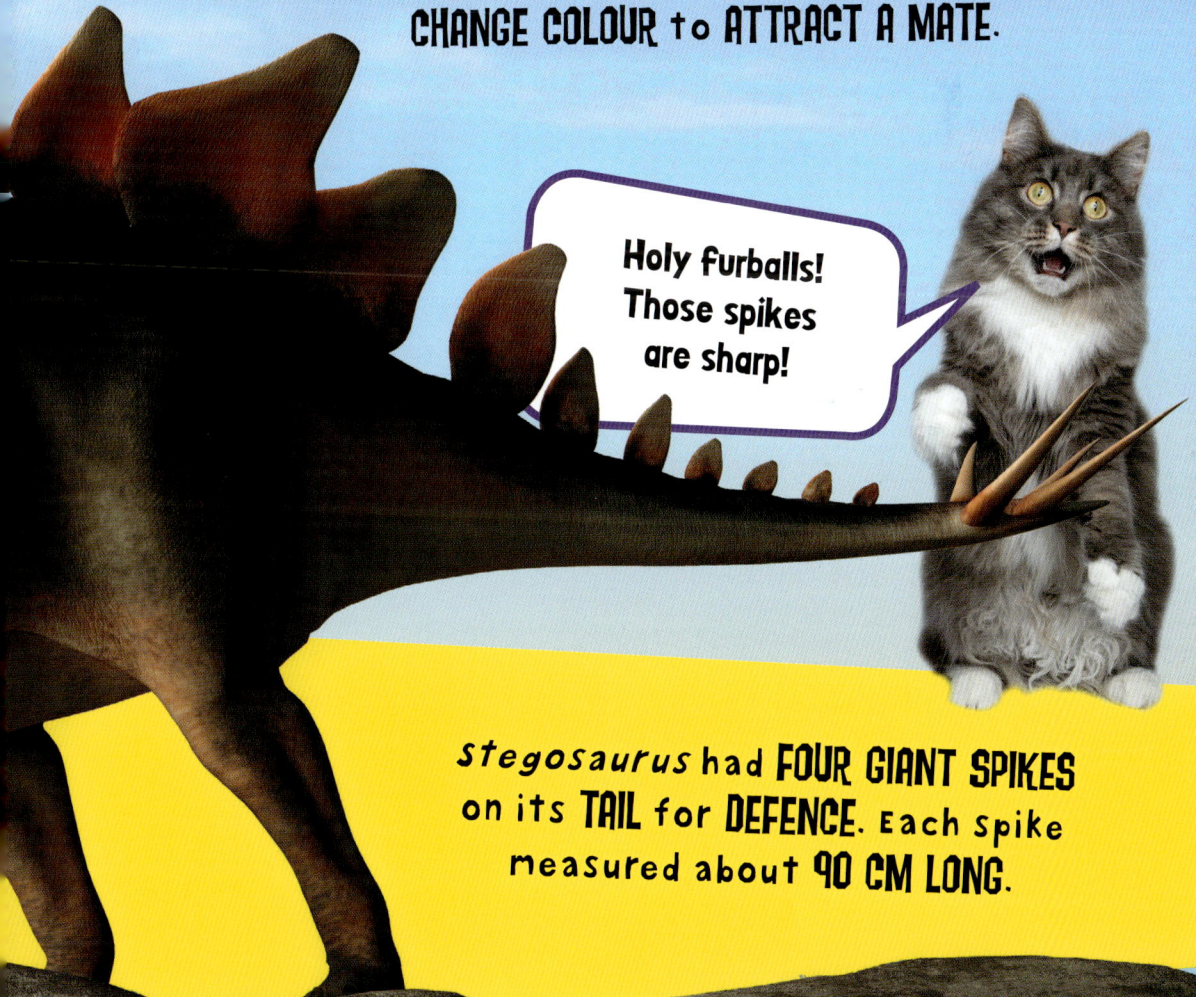

Holy furballs! Those spikes are sharp!

Stegosaurus had FOUR GIANT SPIKES on its TAIL for DEFENCE. Each spike measured about 90 CM LONG.

Stegosaurus's **FRONT LEGS** were **SHORTER** than its **BACK LEGS**, so its head was quite **CLOSE TO THE GROUND.** It fed on **LOW PLANTS,** such as ferns and mosses.

Think I'll stick to fishies.

Wait, what?

STEGOSAURUS HAD THE SMALLEST BRAIN OF ANY DINOSAUR COMPARED TO ITS SIZE. STEGOSAURUS WAS ABOUT AS LONG AS A MALE AFRICAN ELEPHANT, BUT ITS BRAIN WAS AS SMALL AS A PLUM!

No way!

OMG!

Gross!

Wow!

Mind-blowing!

BARYONYX

This **LARGE THEROPOD** mostly **ATE FISH**.

Baryonyx's **LONG JAWS** had a similar shape to those of a **MODERN CROCODILE**. They were filled with **SHARP TEETH** to **GRAB SLIPPERY PREY**.

Baryonyx used its **MASSIVE CLAWS** to **HOOK FISH** out of the water.

Pass it over, I'm starving!

Baryonyx also **HUNTED** and **ATE OTHER DINOSAURS**. One **FOSSILISED** *Baryonyx* has the **REMAINS** of a **YOUNG IGUANODON** in its **STOMACH**.

36

BARYONYX's THUMB CLAWS WERE 30 CM LONG! ITS MASSIVE CLAWS INSPIRED ITS NAME, WHICH MEANS 'HEAVY CLAW'.

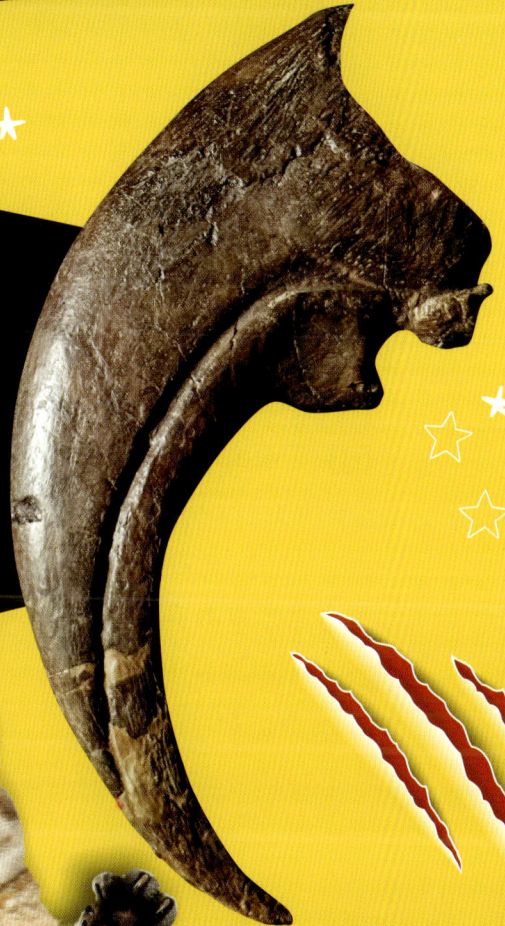

Call that a claw?

No way!

OMG!

Gross!

Wow!

Mind-blowing!

37

IGUANODON

IGUANODON was a **LARGE, HEAVY ORNITHOPOD.** Its **WEIGHT** was mainly **SUPPORTED** by its long, muscular **BACK LEGS** and **BALANCED** out by its **TAIL.**

IGUANODON could **SWITCH BACK AND FORTH** between **WALKING ON TWO LEGS** or on **ALL FOURS.**

When *Iguanodon* walked on **ALL FOURS,** its **THREE MIDDLE FINGERS** acted like a **HOOF** and could **SUPPORT SOME** of its **WEIGHT.**

Iguanodon was a **HERBIVORE**. Its **TEETH** had **SERRATED EDGES** to cut through **LEAVES**. It also had a **HARD BEAK** made out of **KERATIN**. This is the same **MATERIAL** that our **NAILS** are made from.

Thumbs up!

Iguanodon is famous for its **LARGE THUMB SPIKES**. These spikes may have been used for **DEFENCE** against **PREDATORS** such as *Baryonyx*, or for **CUTTING** into **TOUGH PLANTS**.

In **1822**, British palaeontologists **MARY** and **GIDEON MANTELL** found **FOSSILISED** *IGUANODON* **TEETH** in **ENGLAND**. At that time, **SCIENTISTS** didn't have a good **UNDERSTANDING** of **PREHISTORIC LIFE** or **DINOSAURS**, but the **MANTELLS** knew that the **TEETH** didn't belong to any **ANIMAL** they **RECOGNISED**.

They **NAMED** this new species *Iguanodon* because **ITS TEETH** looked like the **TEETH** of **MODERN IGUANAS**. It was one of the **FIRST DINOSAUR SPECIES** to be **NAMED** and **IDENTIFIED**.

EARLY DRAWINGS OF IGUANODON LOOK VERY DIFFERENT TO MODERN ONES, BECAUSE SCIENTISTS USED TO BELIEVE THAT IGUANODON'S THUMB SPIKE WAS A HORN!

What were they thinking?!

No way!

OMG!

Gross!

Wow!

Mind-blowing!

DEINONYCHUS

Deinonychus was a **FIERCE PREDATOR** that attacked with the **LONG CLAWS** on its **HANDS** and **FEET**.

Deinonychus **PROBABLY HUNTED IN GROUPS,** but the **TEAMWORK ENDED** as soon as the **PREY WAS KILLED**. Any smaller *Deinonychus* that got in the way while feeding would have been **ATTACKED** or even **KILLED**.

That's it! Take him down!

Groups of *Deinonychus* hunted larger dinosaurs such as *Tenontosaurus*.

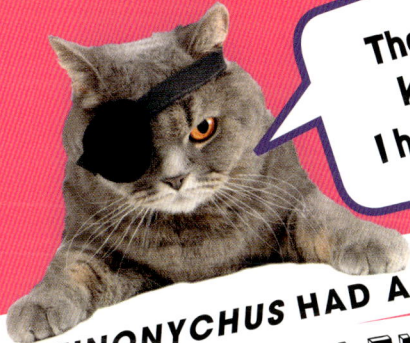

They say curiosity killed the cat — I had a lucky escape.

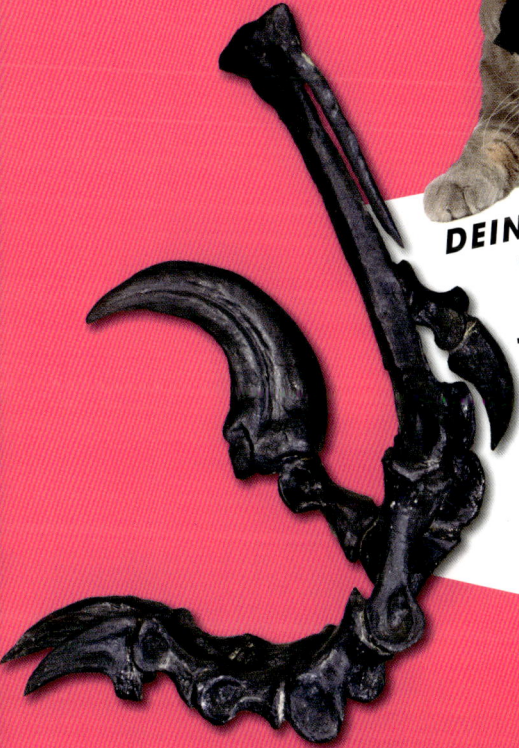

DEINONYCHUS HAD A PARTICULARLY LONG KILLING CLAW ON THE SECOND TOE OF EACH FOOT. IT HELD THIS CLAW OFF THE GROUND WHILE RUNNING TO KEEP IT SHARP!

Wow!

No way!

OMG!

Gross!

Mind-blowing!

YUTYRANNUS

This dinosaur is the **LARGEST FEATHERED ANIMAL** that ever lived!

YUTYRANNUS was an **EARLY RELATIVE** of **TYRANNOSAURUS**. Its feathers were up to **20 CM LONG!** They may have helped to keep **YUTYRANNUS** warm.

Good thing we've got these feathers - I'm freezing!

Yutyrannus fossils have been found in north-eastern China. This area might have had a cold climate in the Early Cretaceous Period.

FACT FILE

Don't go getting any ideas!

YUTYRANNUS'S **FEATHERS** WERE **STRINGY**, LIKE THE **FUZZY** DOWN OF A BABY CHICK!

Wow!

No way!

OMG!

Gross!

Mind-blowing!

45

GALLIMIMUS

This **SUPER-SPEEDY FEATHERY** dino looked and **MOVED** like an **OSTRICH**!

GALLIMIMUS was probably an **OMNIVORE**. It ate **LEAVES** and **SEEDS**, and used its **LONG NECK** to reach **SMALL PREY** on the ground.

Hey guys, wait for me!

Larger **THEROPODS** also preyed on **GALLIMIMUS**, which used its **SPEED** to **ESCAPE**.

FACT FILE

JUST LIKE MODERN **OSTRICHES**, **GALLIMIMUS** WAS A VERY **FAST SPRINTER!** IT WAS PROBABLY ONE OF THE **SPEEDIEST DINOSAURS!**

Can't catch me!

Wow! No way! OMG! Gross! Mind-blowing!

47

ANKYLOSAURUS

Back, head, tail and even eyelids — nearly every part of *ANKYLOSAURUS* was **PROTECTED** by its **ARMOUR!**

ANKYLOSAURUS had **BONY PLATES** set into its **THICK SKIN**. It was also covered in **BONY KNOBS** and **SPIKES**.

Call that armour?!

It would have been **VERY HARD** for **PREDATORS** to bite through **ANKYLOSAURUS'S ARMOUR.** The only part of *Ankylosaurus's* body that they would have been able to **ATTACK** was its **SOFT STOMACH.**

Not MY soft tummy!

Bet mine is softer!

The **END** of Ankylosaurus's **TAIL** was a **CLUB** made out of **SOLID BONE**. It could **SWING** its tail at **PREDATORS** to **DEFEND** itself.

Watch out back there!

One step closer and I'll give you something to roar about!

A **LARGE** ANKYLOSAURUS MAY HAVE BEEN ABLE TO **HIT PREDATORS** SO **HARD** WITH ITS **TAIL CLUB** THAT IT **SHATTERED** THEIR **BONES!**

OMG!

No way!

Gross!

Wow!

Mind-blowing!

VELOCIRAPTOR

VELOCIRAPTOR was only about the **SIZE** of a **TURKEY**, but it was still a **DEADLY PREDATOR!**

Once **VELOCIRAPTOR** reached its **PREY**, it probably used its **LONG CLAWS** to **PIN IT DOWN.** It then used its **SHARP, SERRATED TEETH** to **KILL** and **EAT** its prey.

Coming your way Kitty!

That's it! Teamwork makes the dream work!

EXPERTS BELIEVE THAT MANY **PREDATORS**, SUCH AS *VELOCIRAPTOR*, HUNTED **IN THE DARK!**

I've got a feline I'm not alone ...

OMG!

No way!

Gross!

Wow!

Mind-blowing!

MAIASAURA

FOSSILS of **MAIASAURA** reveal that they were **EXCELLENT PARENTS!**

Maiasaura lived in **LARGE HERDS**. They probably **MIGRATED** and **RETURNED** to the **SAME PLACES** every year to **LAY EGGS** in **NESTS**.

Mum! Mum! Mum! Mum!

After their **YOUNG HATCHED**, Maiasaura brought **FOOD** to the **NEST** for them to **EAT**. The **BABIES** joined their **PARENTS** in the **HERD** when they **GREW UP**.

FACT FILE

- **LIVED:** Late Cretacious Period
- **LENGTH:** 9 m
- **WEIGHT:** 2,500 kg

MAIASAURA USED ROTTING LEAVES TO KEEP ITS EGGS WARM!

Snuggly but smelly!

Maiasaura was too heavy to sit on top of the eggs!

No judgement here!

No way!

OMG!

Gross!

Wow!

Mind-blowing!

SPINOSAURUS

This **MASSIVE PREDATOR** was at **HOME** on **LAND** and in the **WATER**.

SPINOSAURUS is **FAMOUS** for the **LONG SAIL** that ran along its **BACK**. Its sail was supported by **LONG, BONY SPINES** that reached **1.8 M LONG**.

FACT FILE

LIVED: Late Cretaceous Period
LENGTH: 18 m
WEIGHT: 4,000 kg

SPINOSAURUS'S SAIL may have been able to **CHANGE COLOUR!** It was probably used to **ATTRACT MATES.**

Love your look!

Did someone say sail?

S7

EXPERTS believe that *SPINOSAURUS* may have **BEEN ABLE** to **SWIM**. Like *BARYONYX*, its **JAWS** and **TEETH** were **ADAPTED** to catch **SLIPPERY FISH**.

Holy carp!

Too close fur comfort – I'm out of here!

Tyrannosaurus

Hey!

Spinosaurus

SPINOSAURUS IS THE LARGEST KNOWN CARNIVOROUS DINOSAUR!

What's up titch?

It was longer than Tyrannosaurus.

No way!

OMG!

Gross!

Wow!

Mind-blowing!

59

PACHYCEPHALOSAURUS

PACHYCEPHALOSAURUS had an **UNUSUAL HEAD!**

The top of **PACHYCEPHALOSAURUS'S SKULL** was **COVERED** in a **DOME** of **SOLID BONE**. This dinosaur also had many **BONY KNOBS** around its **HEAD**.

Pachycephalosaurus had very **STRONG BACK LEGS** and **SMALL, UNDERDEVELOPED FRONT LEGS.**

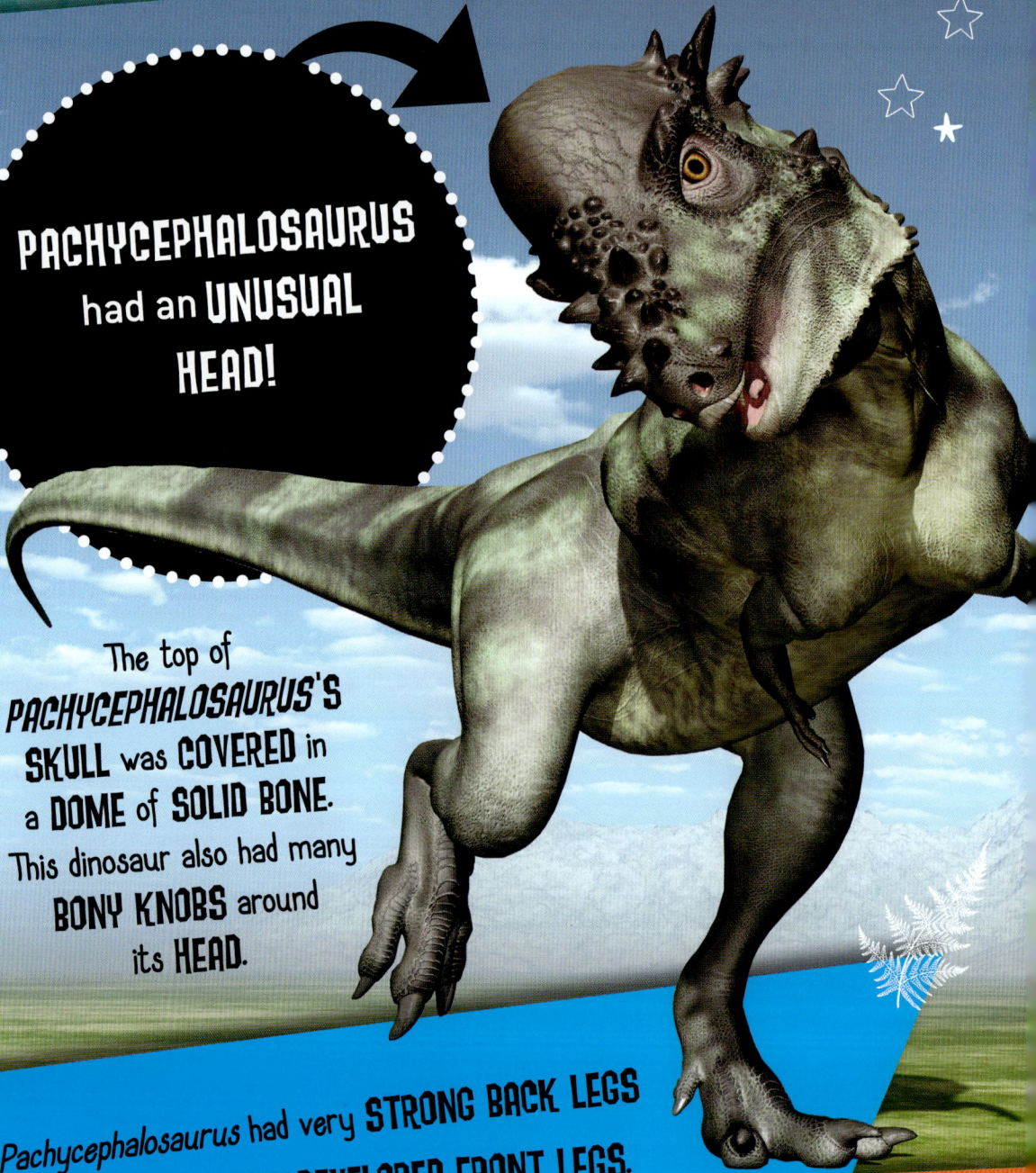

FACT FILE

LIVED: Late Cretaceous Period
LENGTH: 8 m
WEIGHT: 3,000 kg

THE TOP OF PACHYCEPHALOSAURUS'S SKULL COULD BE UP TO 23 CM THICK! THAT'S ABOUT THE LENGTH OF AN AVERAGE ADULT MAN'S FOOT!

Blech! Think I'll use a ruler next time.

A ruler? I've got one somewhere ...

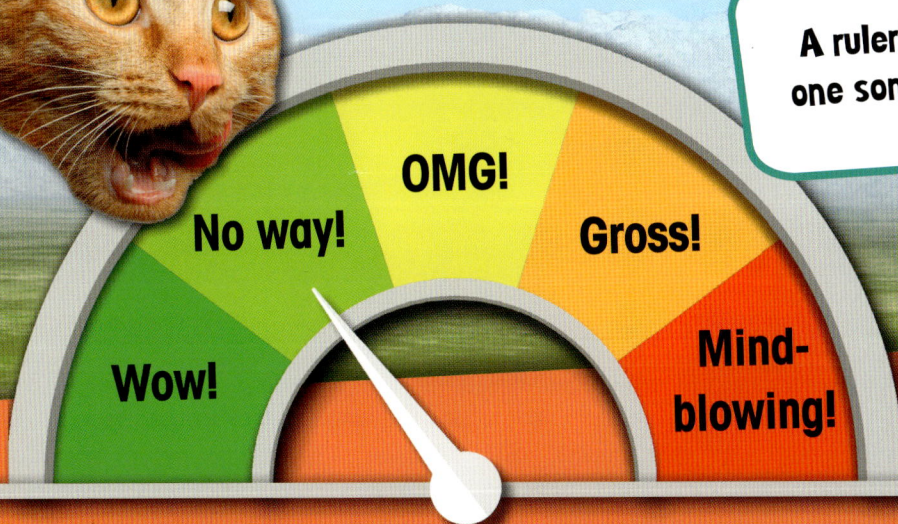

Wow!

No way!

OMG!

Gross!

Mind-blowing!

TYRANNOSAURUS

HUGE, strong and fierce — *TYRANNOSAURUS* was the **ULTIMATE PREDATOR!**

I'm a scaredy cat — get me out of here!

FACT FILE

- **LIVED**: Late Cretaceous Period
- **LENGTH**: 12 m
- **WEIGHT**: 7,000 kg

TYRANNOSAURUS'S massive jaws held **60 TEETH**. Some of its teeth were **20 CM LONG**, which is about the **LENGTH OF A FORK!**

Tyrannosaurus's **TEETH** could **CRUNCH** through **BONE**. It **SWALLOWED** chunks of **MEAT WHOLE** without **CHEWING** them.

We're gonna need a bigger toothbrush.

Tyrannosaurus's **TINY ARMS** probably **COULDN'T** have **REACHED** its **MOUTH** or held on to **PREY**. However, its **JAWS** were so **STRONG** that this **DIDN'T REALLY MATTER!**

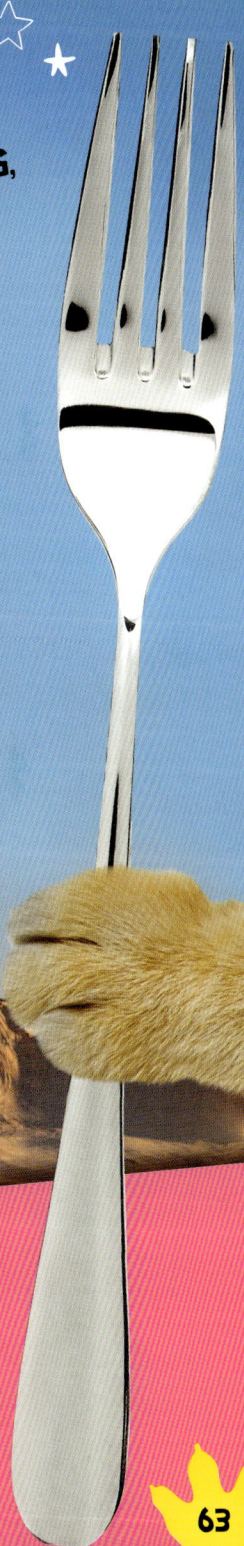

63

TYRANNOSAURUS had an EXCELLENT sense of SMELL, which it used to FIND its PREY. It HUNTED LIVE ANIMALS and also scavenged DEAD BODIES.

I smell dinner!

TYRANNOSAURUS'S BITE WAS THREE TIMES MORE POWERFUL THAN THAT OF A LION!

Holy mackerel!

Wow! | No way! | OMG! | Gross! | Mind-blowing!

TRICERATOPS

The name **TRICERATOPS** means 'three-horned face'. It's easy to see how it got its name!

TRICERATOPS had one **SHORT HORN** on its **NOSE** and two **LONG HORNS** above its **EYES**. The horns above its eyes had **SHARP TIPS** and could measure over **I M LONG!**

frill

Triceratops's horns and frill were part of its skeleton.

I've got a bone to pick with you, Dino!

66

Triceratops's **BONY NECK FRILL** may have acted like a **SHIELD** to **PROTECT** its **NECK** from **PREDATORS**. It also could have helped to **ATTRACT** a **MATE**.

Frilled to meet you!

TRICERATOPS was one of the **LAST LARGE DINOSAURS** to **EVOLVE**. It **LIVED** in the last **3 MILLION YEARS** of the **CRETACEOUS PERIOD**, at the same time as *TYRANNOSAURUS*.

Ever get the feeling that something bad is about to happen?

INCOMING!!

THE LARGEST *TRICERATOPS* SKULLS MEASURE NEARLY 3 M LONG! THAT'S AS LONG AS A MALE INDIAN TIGER!

It's okay Tigey, you're still a giant to me!

Thanks young'un.

Wow!

No way!

OMG!

Gross!

Mind-blowing!

THE END OF THE

DINOSAURS RULED EARTH for **MILLIONS** of **YEARS**, before suddenly **DISAPPEARING 66 MILLION YEARS AGO**.

Wait ... what? What happened?

DIFFERENT dinosaur species **CAME** and **WENT** throughout the **MESOZOIC ERA**. Some dinosaurs **EVOLVED** into **NEW SPECIES** that were better **ADAPTED** to their **ENVIRONMENT**, while others became **EXTINCT**.

Can I evolve some fangs, like now?!

DINOSAURS

Oh no! Not me too?

FOSSILS show that **ALL DINOSAURS**, apart from **BIRDS**, became **EXTINCT 66 MILLION YEARS AGO**. They weren't the only species to **VANISH. PTEROSAURS** (see pages 76-81) and **LARGE MARINE REPTILES** (see pages 82-89) also **DIED OUT** at the same time, in a **MASS EXTINCTION** event.

Your fangs sir ...

Paw dinos.

Many **SCIENTISTS** agree that the **EXTINCTION** of the **DINOSAURS** was caused by a **MASSIVE METEORITE** that **CRASHED** into **EARTH**.

I'm not taking a chance on my nine lives!

MANY **SCIENTISTS** BELIEVE THAT A MASSIVE **150-KM-WIDE CRATER** OFF THE COAST OF **MEXICO** IS THE SITE OF THE **METEORITE COLLISION** THAT **WIPED OUT** THE **DINOSAURS!**

Spot it?

Right here boss!

OMG!

No way!

Gross!

Wow!

Mind-blowing!

The **COLLISION** created **HUGE CLOUDS** of **DUST** and **GAS** that **BLOCKED LIGHT** from the **SUN.** Earth became **DARKER** and **COLDER**, and plants could not grow well. There was **NOT ENOUGH FOOD** to support **LARGE ANIMALS**, and so they **DIED OUT.**

The **ONLY ANIMALS** to **SURVIVE** the **MASS EXTINCTION** event were **SMALL MAMMALS, REPTILES, BIRDS, AMPHIBIANS** and **FISH.** Some of these species are the **ANCESTORS** of the **ANIMALS** that are **ALIVE TODAY.**

So glad your fishy ancestors survived!

74

James? Clare? Where is everyone?

PTEROSAURS

DINOSAURS weren't the only PREHISTORIC REPTILES!

FLYING REPTILES called PTEROSAURS lived throughout the MESOZOIC ERA. They became EXTINCT at the SAME TIME as the DINOSAURS.

Pteranodon (a type of pterosaur)

Pterosaurs rule, dinosaurs drool!

PTEROSAURS were the first VERTEBRATES to take to the SKIES. Their WINGS were made of a STRETCHED MEMBRANE of SKIN, similar to modern BAT WINGS.

PTEROSAURS OFTEN HAD **BRIGHT, COLOURFUL CRESTS!**

Tapejara

The colours! The shapes! C'est magnifique!

Can you paint me next?

No way!

OMG!

Gross!

Wow!

Mind-blowing!

RHAMPHORHYNCHUS

EARLY PTEROSAURS, such as **RHAMPHORHYNCHUS**, were quite **SMALL** with long **TAILS**.

long wing finger

Pterosaurs' wings were supported by one extremely long finger. **RHAMPHORHYNCHUS'S** wing finger was three times as long as its body!

'Sup toothy?

FACT FILE

WE KNOW THAT RHAMPHORHYNCHUS ATE FISH BECAUSE FISH BONES HAVE BEEN FOUND IN ITS FOSSILISED POO!

Why do I always get the claw-ful jobs!

No way!

OMG!

Wow!

Gross!

Mind-blowing!

QUETZALCOATLUS

QUETZALCOATLUS wasn't just the **LARGEST** pterosaur ... it was the **LARGEST FLYING ANIMAL** of all time!

QUETZALCOATLUS GLIDED and **SOARED** across the **SKIES** like a huge **BIRD OF PREY**. It also **MOVED WELL** on **LAND**. It **FOLDED** up its **WINGS** and hunted **PREY** on all fours.

QUETZALCOATLUS didn't have any **TEETH,** so it **SWALLOWED** its **PREY** of fish and small dinosaurs **WHOLE.**

Pick on someone your own size!

FACT FILE

LIVED: Late Cretaceous Period
LENGTH: 10–11 m
WINGSPAN: 10–12 m

Can't ... look ... down!

QUETZALCOATLUS WAS AS TALL AS A GIRAFFE AND HAD THE WINGSPAN OF A SMALL AIRCRAFT!

Is it a bird? Is it a plane?

No way!

OMG!

Gross!

Wow!

Mind-blowing!

PREHISTORIC SEA ANIMALS

OCEANS were FULL of LIFE in the MESOZOIC ERA!

MESOZOIC SEA CREATURES included FISH, SHARKS, AMMONITES and MASSIVE MARINE REPTILES, such as ICHTHYOSAURS and PLESIOSAURS.

Kronosaurus was a massive ocean plesiosaur that hunted ammonites, large fish and other marine reptiles.

Ammonites are related to modern-day octopuses and squids. They mostly became extinct at the same time as the dinosaurs.

Hey! Paws off my lunch!

THE JURASSIC FISH **LEEDSICHTHYS** WAS *LARGER* THAN **ANY OTHER ANIMAL** IN THE **SEA** AND HAD OVER **40,000 TEETH!**

I'm purr-fectly relaxed!

But don't worry – *Leedsichthys* was a gentle giant! It used its teeth to sieve tiny animals from the water.

Wow!

No way!

OMG!

Gross!

Mind-blowing!

83

ICHTHYOSAURS

ICHTHYOSAURS looked a bit like **DOLPHINS**, but they were actually **REPTILES**!

However, like **DOLPHINS**, **ICHTHYOSAURS** and all other marine reptiles **BREATHED AIR**. Their **ANCESTORS** originally lived on **LAND**. When **ICHTHYOSAURS** moved into the **OCEANS**, they adapted to **LIFE** in the **WATER** by becoming more **STREAMLINED**. Over time, their **ARMS** and **LEGS** changed into **FLIPPERS**.

I'm ready for life underwater too!

ONE SPECIES OF ICHTHYOSAUR, TEMNODONTOSAURUS, HAD EYES THAT WERE BIGGER THAN FOOTBALLS!

My hero!

Wow!

No way!

OMG!

Gross!

Mind-blowing!

PLESIOSAURS

Some **PLESIOSAURS** had very **LONG NECKS!**

PLESIOSAUR NECKS weren't very **FLEXIBLE**, but they could probably **DIP DOWN** to **CATCH FISH** or **GRAB SHELLFISH** from the **SEABED**.

Quite claws-e enough!

SOME SPECIES of plesiosaur were the **PREY** of **LARGER MARINE REPTILES**. Others were **APEX PREDATORS** and **HUNTED** other **LARGE MARINE ANIMALS**.

THE PLESIOSAUR *ELASMOSAURUS* HAD OVER 70 BONES IN ITS 6.5-M-LONG NECK!

I win!

I only have seven!

Not exactly neck and neck ...

Wow!

No way!

OMG!

Gross!

Mind-blowing!

MOSASAURS

MOSASAURS ruled the seas in the **LATE CRETACEOUS PERIOD** after **ICHTHYOSAURS** and some **PLESIOSAURS** became **EXTINCT**.

Mosasaurs had a **VARIED DIET**, including **TURTLES**, **AMMONITES, FISH, SHARKS, SEA BIRDS** ... and even **OTHER MOSASAURS!**

They could **OPEN** their **JAWS** really **WIDE** to fit in **LARGE PREY**, in a similar way to **SNAKES** today.

Reverse! Reverse!

THE **LARGEST** SPECIES OF **MOSASAUR** COULD REACH **17 M LONG**, WHILE THE **SMALLEST** WERE JUST **1 M LONG!**

This isn't the mini mosasaur I had in mind!

Just keep swimming!

No way!

OMG!

Gross!

Wow!

Mind-blowing!

EARLY AMPHIBIANS AND REPTILES

AMPHIBIANS were the first FOUR-LEGGED LAND ANIMALS!

Just under 120 MILLION YEARS before the MESOZOIC ERA, some species of FISH evolved for LIFE out of the WATER. Their FINS turned into FEET and they could BREATHE AIR. These were the FIRST AMPHIBIANS!

Eryops was a big prehistoric amphibian that was around 2 m long.

Is it our turn yet?

You're the best!

Best family ever!

Thanks guys!

DINOSAURS AND ALL MODERN REPTILES, AMPHIBIANS, BIRDS AND MAMMALS, INCLUDING HUMANS, ARE DESCENDANTS OF THESE PREHISTORIC AMPHIBIANS!

No way!

OMG!

Gross!

Wow!

Mind-blowing!

THE FIRST BIRDS

BIRDS are the only SURVIVING DESCENDANTS of DINOSAURS!

Stay ... still ... almost ...

By the **JURASSIC PERIOD**, some small **THEROPODS** had evolved **BIRD-LIKE FEATURES**, such as **FLUFFY FEATHERS** and **WINGS**. However, they may **NOT** have been able to **FLY WELL**.

The **FIRST BIRDS** appeared in the **CRETACEOUS PERIOD**. They could **FLY** well, and had **BEAKS** and **PROPER FEATHERS**. These were the species that **SURVIVED** the **MASS EXTINCTION** that **KILLED** the **DINOSAURS**, and evolved into **MODERN BIRDS**.

Confuciusornis was a crow-sized bird that lived in the Early Cretaceous Period.

MANY **PREHISTORIC BIRDS** WERE **HUGE!**
DROMORNIS WAS A **GIANT FLIGHTLESS**
BIRD THAT **WEIGHED** UP TO **500 KG**
— AROUND AS
MUCH AS **SIX**
ADULT MEN!

Now that's
a seriously
large lunch!

Dromornis
lived after the
time of the
dinosaurs.

No way!

OMG!

Gross!

Wow!

Mind-
blowing!

PREHISTORIC MAMMALS

The **FIRST MAMMALS EVOLVED** in the **TRIASSIC PERIOD**.

During the time of the **DINOSAURS**, most **MAMMALS** were **SMALL** – about the **SIZE** of a **MODERN RAT**.

Megazostrodon probably ate insects and worms.

It wasn't until **DINOSAURS** became **EXTINCT** that **MAMMALS** grew **LARGER**. They **FILLED** the **GAP** that **DINOSAURS** left behind and became the **DOMINANT LAND ANIMALS**.

Daddy?

Smilodon was a sabre-toothed cat that died out about 10,000 years ago. Its front fangs were up to 20 cm long, which is as long as some *Tyrannosaurus* teeth!

FOSSILS

ALMOST EVERYTHING we know about what **DINOSAURS LOOKED LIKE** and how they **BEHAVED** comes from **FOSSILS!**

Good thing you're just a rock!

A **FOSSIL** is the **PRESERVED REMAINS** of a **PREHISTORIC LIVING THING**. It **ISN'T** the same as the **REMAINS** themselves – it's a **ROCK COPY** of the remains that looks **EXACTLY** the **SAME**.

Sinosauropteryx had a ginger and white striped tail!

PIGMENT CELLS FROM FOSSILISED DINOSAUR FEATHERS AND SKIN CAN TELL US WHAT COLOUR DINOSAURS WERE!

Tail stripes? I invented those darling!

Wow!

No way!

OMG!

Gross!

Mind-blowing!

97

Only a very **SMALL NUMBER** of **PREHISTORIC ANIMALS** and **PLANTS** have been **PRESERVED** as fossils. The **CONDITIONS** have to be **EXACTLY RIGHT** for **FOSSILISATION** to take place.

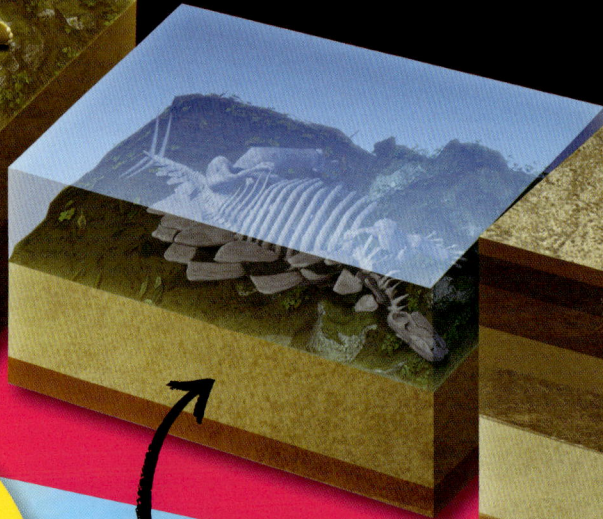

The animal's flesh rots away, leaving just the hard body parts, such as bones and teeth.

The body is covered by mud or sand, usually underwater.

More layers of mud and sand build up over time.

Dave! I think I've found something!

The layers of mud and sand turn into sedimentary rock.

The hard body parts are replaced by minerals and turn to rock.

Millions of years later, the rock wears away, revealing the fossil underneath.

I think we've found something too!

99

We can also **LEARN** about **DINOSAURS** from **TRACE FOSSILS**. These **AREN'T** fossils of **BODY PARTS**. They are **FOSSILISED RECORDS** of **DINOSAUR BEHAVIOUR**, such as their **FOOTPRINTS**, **NESTS**, **EGGS** and even their **POO**.

Eww!

A **FOSSILISED PREHISTORIC POO** is known as a **COPROLITE**. **PALAEONTOLOGISTS** study coprolites to find out **WHAT DINOSAURS ATE**.

Who's been eating my kibble?

Ahem ...

THE **LARGEST DINOSAUR** **FOOTPRINT** EVER FOUND MEASURES **1.7 M LONG!** A **SHORT HUMAN ADULT** COULD **FIT INSIDE** THE FOOTPRINT!

> Or two cats!

Wow!

No way!

OMG!

Gross!

Mind-blowing!

AMBER

PREHISTORIC REMAINS are sometimes **TRAPPED** in **AMBER!**

AMBER is **FOSSILISED TREE RESIN.** When the resin was **FRESH** and **STICKY,** prehistoric **INSECTS, SPIDERS** and **SMALL ANIMALS** sometimes got stuck to it. Over **MILLIONS OF YEARS,** the **RESIN** turned into **AMBER, TRAPPING** the animals **INSIDE FOREVER.**

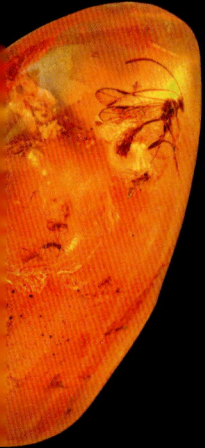

HELP! I've been trapped in here for meow-llions of years!

Blue is best!

blue amber

MOST **AMBER** IS **YELLOWY-BROWN**, BUT IT CAN ALSO BE VERY **PALE YELLOW, WHITE, DARK RED, BLACK** AND EVEN **BLUE!**

I beg to differ, Bluey!

OMG!

No way!

Gross!

Wow!

Mind-blowing!

DINOSAURS REACT

Now it's our turn!

Wait, what? That's our job!

Did you know that cats spend 30 to 50 per cent of their time awake washing themselves?

What's wrong with keeping clean?!

I'm feline confused by all these long dinosaur names – HELP!

I've got a dino-mite guide just for you!

PURR-NUNCIATION GUIDE

Alamosaurus (ah-la-mow-SORE-us)
Albertaceratops (al-bert-a-SER-ra-tops)
Allosaurus (AL-oh-sore-us)
Ankylosaurus (an-KEEL-oh-sore-us)
Apatosaurus (ah-PAT-oh-sore-us)
Archaeopteryx (ark-ee-OPT-er-ix)
Argentinosaurus (AR-gent-ee-no-sore-us)
Baryonyx (bah-ree-ON-icks)
Brachiosaurus (BRAK-ee-oh-sore-us)
Coelophysis (seel-OH-fie-sis)
Compsognathus (komp-sog-NATH-us)
Confuciusornis (kon-few-shu-SOR-niss)
Deinonychus (die-NON-eye-kuss)
Dilophosaurus (die-LOAF-oh-sore-us)
Diplodocus (DIP-lo-DOH-cus or dip-LOD-er-cus)
Elasmosaurus (eh-laz-muh-SORE-us)
Eryops (EH-ree-ops)
Gallimimus (gah-lee-MEEM-us)

Hadrosaurus (HAD-row-sore-us)

ichthyosaur (ICK-thee-oh-sore)

Iguanodon (ig-WHA-noh-don)

Kentrosaurus (ken-TROH-sore-us)

Kosmoceratops (coz-mo-SER-ra-tops)

Kronosaurus (crow-no-SORE-us)

Leedsichthys (leed-SICK-thiss)

Maiasaura (my-ah-SORE-ah)

Mamenchisaurus (mah-men-chi-SORE-us)

Megazostrodon (meg-uh-ZOSS-truh-don)

Microraptor (MIKE-row-rap-tor)

mosasaur (MOZE-uh-sore)

Pachycephalosaurus (pack-ee-KEF-ah-lo-sore-us)

Parasaurolophus (pa-ra-saw-ROL-off-us)

plesiosaur (PLEE-zee-oh-sore)

Pteranodon (terr-AN-oh-don)

pterosaur (TERR-oh-sore)

Quetzalcoatlus (ket-zel-KWAT-a-lus)

Rhamphorhynchus (RAM-four-ink-us)

Sinosauropteryx (sine-oh-sore-OPT-ter-icks)

Smilodon (SMILE-uh-don)

Spinosaurus (SPINE-oh-sore-us)

Stegosaurus (STEG-oh-sore-us)

Styracosaurus (sty-RAK-oh-sore-us)

Tapejara (TAH-pe-jar-uh)

Temnodontosaurus (tem-no-DONT-uh-sore-us)

Tenontosaurus (ten-ON-toe-sore-us)

Triceratops (tri-SER-ra-tops)

Tyrannosaurus (tie-RAN-oh-sore-us)

Velociraptor (vel-OSS-ee-rap-tor)

Yutyrannus (YOU-tee-ran-us)

CLAW-SSARY

amber - fossilised tree resin

amphibian - an animal that lays eggs in water, but can live on land or in water

ancestor - an animal that is related to another type of animal that lived later in time

apex predator - an animal with no natural predators

cannibal - an animal that eats other animals of its own species

carnivore - an animal that only eats meat

continent - one of the main pieces of land on Earth

crater - a round hole in the ground

crest - a growth of skin, fur or feathers on an animal's head

dominant - stronger and more powerful than anything else in the area

era - a period of Earth's history based on the age of layers of sedimentary rock

evolve - to change and develop gradually over time

fossil - the shape of something that has been preserved in rock for a very long time

herbivore - an animal that only eats plants

herd - a large group of animals that live and feed together

mammal - an animal that feeds its young on milk from its own body, and usually gives birth to live young

mass extinction - a period in which many species of living thing die and stop existing

mate - a reproductive partner

membrane - a thin piece of skin

meteorite - a piece of space rock that has landed on Earth

migrate - to travel to another place, usually when the season changes

omnivore - an animal that eats meat and plants

palaeontologist - someone who studies dinosaurs and prehistoric life

period - a length of time within an era

pigment - a substance that gives something a colour

predator - an animal that kills and eats other animals

prehistoric - describes the time before written records

prey - an animal eaten by other animals

reproduce - to produce new plants

reptile - an animal that lays eggs and uses heat from the Sun to keep warm

sauropod - a type of huge dinosaur that had a long neck and ate plants

scavenge - to feed on dead and decaying animals

sedimentary rock - rock that forms from layers of sediment being pressed together over time

serrated - with a row of sharp points

spore - a type of cell produced by plants without seeds that is able to grow into a new plant

theropod - a type of dinosaur that was usually a predator and that had sharp teeth and claws

vertebrate - an animal with a backbone, such as fish or mammals

wingspan - the distance between the tips of the wings of an animal

FUR-THER INFORMATION

BOOKS

Dinosaurs (Prehistoric Life)
by Claire Hibbert (Franklin Watts, 2019)

Dino-sorted series
by Sonya Newland and Izzi Howell (Franklin Watts, 2021)

Time Trails: Dinosaurs
by Liz Gogerly, Rob Hunt and Oivind Hovland (Franklin Watts, 2019)

WEBSITES

www.nhm.ac.uk/discover/what-dinosaur-are-you.html
Take a quiz to find out what kind of dinosaur you are!

kids.nationalgeographic.com/animals/prehistoric
Learn more about different types of dinosaur.

www.dkfindout.com/uk/dinosaurs-and-prehistoric-life/
prehistoric-reptiles/
Find out about other prehistoric reptiles.

KITTEN-DEX